WHY SHOULD I SHARE?

W
HODDER
Wayland

an imprint of Hodder Children's Books

WHY SHOULD I?

WHY SHOULD I Eat Well?
WHY SHOULD I Help?
WHY SHOULD I Listen?
WHY SHOULD I Share?

Published in Great Britain in 2001 by Hodder Wayland,
an imprint of Hodder Children's Books
© Copyright 2001 Hodder Wayland

Commissioning editor: Alex Woolf
Editor: Liz Gogerly
Designer: Jean Wheeler
Digital Colour: Carl Gordon

British Library Cataloguing in Publication Data
Llewellyn, Claire
Why should I share?
1.Sharing - Juvenile literature
I.Title II.Share
302.1'4

ISBN 0 7502 3643 4

Printed and bound in Italy by G. Canale & C.Sp.A., Turin

Hodder Children's Books
A division of Hodder Headline Limited
338 Euston Road, London NW1 3BH

WHY SHOULD I SHARE?

Written by Claire Llewellyn

Illustrated by Mike Gordon

HODDER
Wayland

an imprint of Hodder Children's Books

Mum was cross with me this morning.
It was all about me not sharing.

Mum said sharing was a kind thing to do. It showed you were thinking about other people. And not just about yourself.

8

She said, 'What do you think will happen if you don't share your toys?'

'No one will ever want to play with you.'

'And guess what will happen if you don't share goodies?'

11

'Your friends won't like you any more.'

'And what do you
think will happen if
you're unkind to Jack
and won't let him
play with the yo-yo?'

'I'll take it away and then nobody will have any fun.'

14

Humph!
I was so mad I went next-door
to see the twins.

Kay and Kathy are my best friends.
They told me they had grown up
sharing.

They said sharing made
things more fun.

The three of us played together
all afternoon.

And I began to see what
they meant.

Sharing was more fun,
and friendlier, too.

Sharing can make
things a whole lot better.
I mean, what's the point of
having a brand new frisbee ...

if you don't
share it with a friend?

And, though it's great to have your own special pet,

it's twice as good to share it with your friends.

Sharing can also be useful.
Some people share things now
and again.

Others share them all the time.

I thought I could try a bit harder to share.
After tea, I was listening to my walkman, and Jack was feeling a bit left out.

So I said, 'Here you can listen, too.'

Oh, Tim – that's sweet of you to share.

Sharing is friendly and
makes people happy.
And there's another good
thing about it too –
once you learn to
share with others ...

they may well
learn to share
with you!

Notes for parents and teachers

Why Should I? and the National Curriculum

The Why Should I? series satisfies a number of requirements for the *Personal, Social and Health Education non-statutory framework at Key Stage 1.* Within the category *Developing confidence and responsibility,* these books will help young readers to recognize what they like and dislike, what is fair and unfair, and what is right and wrong; to think about themselves, learn from their experiences and recognize what they are good at. Under *Developing a healthy, safer lifestyle,* some of the titles in this series will help to teach children how to make simple choices that improve their health and well-being, to maintain personal hygiene, and to learn rules for, and ways of, keeping safe, including basic road safety. Under *Developing good relationships and respecting the differences between people,* reading these books will help children to recognize how their behaviour affects other people, to listen to other people and play and work cooperatively, and that family and friends should care for each other.

About Why Should I Share?

Why Should I Share? is intended to be an enjoyable book which discusses the importance of sharing. Sharing is often a difficult thing for children to do. A variety of situations throughout this book explore the ways in which sharing can benefit people.

Sharing is a way of giving. Taking turns with a toy or sharing sweets and equipment encourages children to develop relationships with others. Working and playing together teaches children to cooperate – with their families, their friends and people at school. It is a way of getting on with others.

Sharing is a way of understanding other people's feelings. Some children find it hard to think of anything outside themselves. Being on the receiving end of someone's generosity (or perhaps selfishness) may help to encourage empathy in children and develop an understanding and knowledge of themselves as individuals.

Sharing encourages children to feel good about themselves. Children should always be praised for sharing. Positive feedback helps to enhance their self-esteem.

Suggestions as you read the book with children

This book is full of examples of times when children succeed or fail to share. As you come across each example, it might be useful to stop and discuss it with children. Are there some things they find hard to share? What are they?

We all like it when people are willing to share with us. Can they think of any times when this has happened to them. What were the circumstances?

Ask the children about what sharing actually means. Why is sharing important? Get them to try to imagine a world where no one shared. Would people be happier or sadder? Encourage them to reflect that they belong to various groups and communities such as their family and school, and that it would be impossible for these groups and communities to function without sharing.

We also share the environment with every other person and animal in the world, and sharing in this case means exercising responsibility.

Suggested follow-up activities

Plan a group task, such as building a model castle, which entails sharing equipment with other pupils or friends.

Children could ask their grandparents or some other older person how they shared things when they were young. During the Second World War, people had to share possessions such as clothes and food so there was enough to go around. Do they think that people used to share more in those days? (History curriculum: Knowledge and understanding of events, people and changes in the past: Pupils should be taught to identify differences between ways of life at different times.)

Play a game in which two pirates have to share out some booty. Draw pictures of a treasure chest, jewellery, treasure map, coins, etc. Can the children share the treasure fairly?

Books to read

Aren't You Lucky? by Laurence and Catherine Anholt (Red Fox, 1995)
The story about the arrival of a new baby brother which explores the subjects of jealousy and sharing with siblings.

Pumpkin Soup by Helen Cooper (Corgi, 1999)
The ups and downs of friendship and sharing are explored in this beautiful and amusing picture book.

This is Our House by Michael Rosen (Heinemann)
A humorous picture book which tackles the subject of sharing and friendship.

Two Can Share, Too (Bear in the Big Blue House) by Janelle Cherrington and Normand Chartier (Simon and Schuster, 1999).